# My Visit to the FIRE STATION

## Sophie Davies
and
## Diana Bentley
Reading Consultant
University of Reading

Photographs by
## Trevor Hill

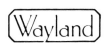

# My Visit

My Visit to the Airport
My Visit to the Birthday Party
My Visit to the Dentist
My Visit to the Doctor
My Visit to the Fire Station
My Visit to the Hospital
My Visit to the Museum
My Visit to the Seaside
My Visit to the Supermarket
My Visit to the Swimming Pool
My Visit to the Theme Park
My Visit to the Zoo

First published in 1990 by
Wayland (Publishers) Ltd
61 Western Road, Hove
East Sussex, BN3 1JD, England

© Copyright 1990 Wayland (Publishers) Limited

**British Library Cataloguing in Publication Data**
Davies, Sophie
  My visit to the fire station.
  1. Fire stations
  I. Title II. Bentley, Diana III. Series
  628.9'25

ISBN 1–85210–835–5

Typeset by Rachel Gibbs, Wayland
Printed and bound by Casterman S.A., Belgium

# Contents

All words that appear in **bold** are explained in the glossary on page 22

# Hello, my name is Simmone.

I am very excited, because Mum is taking me to visit a fire station.

My friend Ian is coming with us. We walk to the fire station.

# The fire officers show us round.

We go in the **cab** of a fire engine. The fire officers are wearing special clothes. The clothes protect them when they go to put out a fire.

I pretend to be the driver of the fire engine.

# This is what happens when there is a fire.

This machine is called a **teleprinter**. When there is a fire, a bell rings at the fire station. A message like this one comes out of the teleprinter. It tells the fire officers where the fire is, and how many fire engines are needed.

A fire officer checks where the fire is on a map.

9

# There is not really a fire this time.

The fire officers pretend there is a fire, just to show us what happens. They put on their special clothes and go to the fire engine.
A fire officer passes a message to the driver. It tells him where the fire is and what the fire officers need to do.

These officers show us the pumps at the back
of the fire engine. This is where the water
comes from to put out a fire. We climb up the
ladders to look.

# We pretend to put out a fire.

You need a lot of water to put out a fire. The fire officers show us two **hoses**, a big one and a little one. They turn the water on. It comes out very fast. Whoosh!

Fires sometimes make lots of smoke and **fumes**, so fire officers wear special masks to help them breathe. This officer has a tank full of air on his back. When he puts the mask on, he can breathe the air from the tank.

# This is a special fire engine.

It has a special cage that can reach up very high. The fire officer in the cage waves down to us.

Now we are hungry. This is the room upstairs where the fire officers have their lunch. We have some lunch with them.

# Fire officers have to be very fit.

They exercise at the gym to keep themselves fit. This officer is lifting heavy weights to make his arms strong. I have a go on the **exercise bicycle**.

Some fire officers like to box to keep themselves fit. This fire officer lets us try on the heavy boxing gloves. We pretend to hit him.

# We try on some helmets.

A fire officer shows us the special clothes he wears when he goes to put out a fire. Look at his big boots!

If the fire officers are upstairs when the fire
bell rings, they come down this sliding pole.
It is quicker than using the stairs.

# The fire officers wave goodbye.

We sit on the front of the fire engine with our yellow helmets on. We had a lovely day at the fire station. When I grow up, I want to be a fire officer.

Now it is time to go home. The fire officers stand by one of their fire engines. They wave goodbye to us, and we wave back.

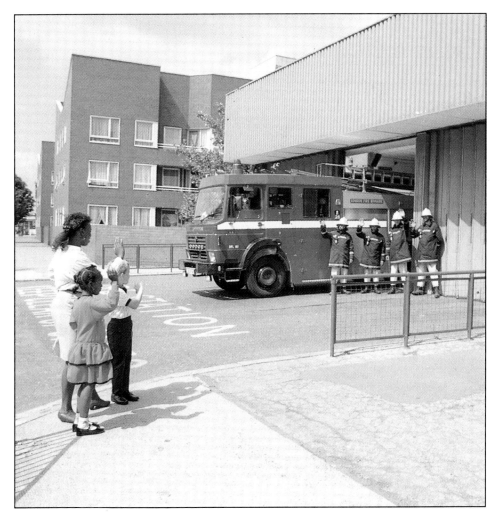

# Glossary

**Cab**  The front of a fire engine or lorry, where the driver sits.

**Exercise bicycle**  A bicycle that is fixed to a stand, so that it can't go anywhere. People use it to keep fit.

**Fumes**  Smoke that is smelly or poisonous.

**Hoses**  Long tubes that spurt water.

**Teleprinter**  A machine that can type out messages that are sent from a long way away.

# Books to read

*Fighting a Fire* Brenda Williams (Kingfisher, 1987)

*The Fire Brigade* Fiona Corbridge (Wayland, 1985)

*Firefighter* Alison Cooper and Diana Bentley (Wayland, 1990)

*Firemen to the Rescue* Catherine De Lasa (Moonlight, 1987)

# Acknowledgements

The author and publishers would like to thank Simmone Davis, Ian Bender and Yvonne Peart; Brian Edwards and the officers of the Blue Watch at the Old Kent Road Fire Station, London, for their help with this book.

# Index